CAMINO

by Sarah B. Kotchian

To my husband, Robert O. Nellums, Jr.,
the best of companions on our shared camino of life
with love and gratitude

Pilgrims Prayer
CODEX CALIXTINUS • 12TH CENTURY

God, You called your servant Abraham from Ur in Chaldea, watching over him in all his wanderings, and guided the Hebrew people as they crossed the desert. Guard these your children who, for love of your Name, make a pilgrimage to Compostela. Be their companion on the way, their guide at the crossroads, their strength in weariness, their defense in dangers, their shelter on the path, their shade in the heat, their light in darkness, their comfort in discouragement, and the firmness of their intentions; that through your guidance, they may arrive safely at the end of their journey and, enriched with grace and virtue, may return to their homes filled with salutary and lasting joy.

—Credencial del Peregrino

Table of Contents

Acknowledgments

Each family member, friend, teacher and life experience shape what we bring to our path and how we walk it. Without being able to name them individually, I thank all of those who have helped prepare the way. With deep gratitude, I wish to also mention more specifically the following:

I thank those who enthusiastically embraced my decision to make a solo pilgrimage in Spain, foremost among them my husband Bob, our daughter Laura, who walked the Camino herself in 2007, and our son Ross. I appreciate the support of our parents, siblings and many friends who encouraged and followed the journey each day as I walked. Spiritual director Sister Geneal Kramer provided a discerning ear and guidance as I deepened my spiritual walk after retirement. My companions at the Hesychia School of Spiritual Direction in Tucson listened and reflected as my language about the Camino changed from thinking about it to planning to do it to declaring that I was going to do it! The Rev. Dr. Kathryn Johnson Cameron, a pastor friend, encouraged me to "just start," in recognition that we never know where those steps will lead us, but that we can follow our sense of calling. She, the Rev. Seth Finch and my Covenant Presbyterian church family gave me a pilgrim blessing and a rainbow ribbon to tie to my pack on the Sunday before I departed. Special friends Jan Haley, Carol Pierce, and Mary Cunnane walked with me during the preceding winter to build up my endurance and to test boots and equipment. Father Michael Fish, Lois McClave and other peregrino friends who had walked the Camino before me helped with guidebooks and advice, as did the ever-helpful staff at REI. Donna O'Neill kept me company with her own painting camino at home.

I carried a journal given to me by long-time friend, Joyce Godwin. She and other family members and friends wrote in the journal in advance, inscribing inspiring messages that I could discover as I proceeded to make my own journal entries during the walk. Those messages were, not surprisingly, not only supportive and loving but also often very appropriate for that particular day. My family and friends and their entries in that journal are life-long treasures.

Many thanks to my brother and sister peregrinos whose paths ran along with mine for some portion of the Camino, to the former pilgrims turned volunteer hospitaleros at the albergues, and to the friendly and generous people of Spain; I learned much from them about myself, about welcoming others, and about God.

Finally, I wish to thank Charlie Kenesson, creative book designer extraordinaria, who understood immediately the significance of the Camino experience and whose artistic talents created a book that helps to convey that experience to others who are walking their own life caminos.   Muchas gracias a todos; vaya con Dios.

Introduction

In March and April of 2012, I made a pilgrimage on the Camino de Santiago in Spain. The desire to walk this path grew in me over five years, after our daughter walked it in 2007. Various activities involving work and family intervened until 2012, when it was possible for me to walk it in an unhurried way.

The Camino de Santiago Compostela has been a route of pilgrimage for more than a thousand years, walked by over one million pilgrims a year at its height in the Middle Ages. Tradition holds that St. James (Santiago) traveled to this city in northwestern Spain in the early Christian era, and that his remains were buried there after his martyrdom in Jerusalem. Due to conflicts in other areas, the city of Santiago was also a safer destination than Rome or Jerusalem for those making a pilgrimage for penance or prayer. Because pilgrims traveled to Santiago from all throughout Europe, there are many routes leading to Santiago. The most commonly walked route is the Camino Francés, beginning in St. Jean Pied de Port, France, continuing over the Pyrenees and westward through the north of Spain. The way is marked by the symbol of the scallop shell and yellow arrows and is approximately 500 miles long. This is the route that I walked. Most pilgrims carry a backpack, and stay at night in the albergues along the route, dormitory-style hostels with bunk beds, often with cooking facilities. At each albergue, the pilgrim receives a stamp on the pilgrim passport, known as the credencial. Many walkers wear a scallop shell, symbol of the Camino, to signify that they are pilgrims. A pilgrim is called a "peregrino," or, in my case, "peregrina," the root words "per agra" describing those who go beyond the fields of home.

Everyone's "camino" is different. Some pilgrims, especially those from Spain, walk one week per year until they complete it. Some walk to Santiago and back to St. Jean. Pilgrims walk the whole route or a portion, taking several days or as long as several months, each according to his or her own circumstances and health. I was advised to go at my own pace, to enjoy each day, and not to hurry. I took this advice, learning to listen to my body and to choose each day how far to walk. My walk took me 39 days, averaging 13 miles per day, with a 40th day at the cathedral in Santiago, reflecting on the journey.

"Why do you make the Camino?" This is a question pilgrims ask one another as they walk along, not unlike some of the large questions we may all eventually ask ourselves in life, such as "Why are we here?" "What are we walking towards?" and, for some, "Whom are you walking for?" In my own case, I was about to turn 59; I wanted to make a solo pilgrimage as a commitment to remaining a strong woman in the next part of life; I looked forward to drawing closer to God, to the time for introspection that comes through the cumulative experience of walking day after day, to the opportunity to notice, and to simply be. There is a saying on the Camino: "Yo no hago el Camino; el Camino me hace a mí:" "I don't make the Camino, the Camino makes me." For it is true that no matter for what reason one walks the Camino—as a spiritual journey, to overcome a difficult challenge, in memory of a loved one—there are other lessons that we also learn, perhaps "not by choice, but by grace," as I write in "Ready Grace." When we greet each other by saying "Buen Camino," we bless the other, not knowing the road he or she has traveled to this point, but knowing that in many ways we share the same road.

The Camino becomes a symbol for all of life as a pilgrimage, with its various stages, its disappointments, sorrows, and joys. While most people are not able to walk a Camino in Spain, all are involved in their own caminos—journeys through family and work challenges, through our own illness or the deaths of those we love, through the trial and error of finding what we love and what holds meaning for us, what feeds us, what calls to us, what brings out our gifts in service to others.

This book of poems grew out of the writing camino I made after my return, a time of reflection on each day walked, on the many blessings and lessons learned in pilgrimage. Each poem can stand on its own, reminding us that each day is a gift, complete in itself. The poems can also be read in sequence, just as the Camino is a deepening experience when walked over consecutive days and weeks. However you choose to read it, it is my hope that this book provides a journey for you as the reader—not only through the eyes of one pilgrim in Spain, but also through your reflections on your own path, bringing more clarity to and gratitude for why you make your camino. All roads bring blessings. Buen Camino!

Threshold

At the threshold I pause
taking in all that is familiar
The woodpile, the front door
I recall the Shehecheyanu,
a Jewish blessing for new beginnings:
"Blessed are you, O Lord our God, Ruler of the Universe
Who has granted us life, and sustained us,
And enabled us to reach this season."

Embracing all that has gone before,
I give thanks.
Then, gathering up all that that I have prepared and
all that has prepared me,
I untie the ropes that hold me in harbor
turn my face
to the new day
and step forward

Transitions

Disembarking into Spain
On the ground once more
I stand surrounded by fellow travelers
Each arrival also a departure
"Equipajes y salida:" "Baggage and way out"
"Puertas:" "Gates"
A choice of what bags to carry
Which door to open.

On the next flight from Madrid to Pamplona
I look down on the landscapes of northern Spain
Unfamiliar landmarks
Snow-capped mountains, farms, land of wine and wind.
In two days I will be walking there
over that snowy pass
Even now the pilgrims walk below
perhaps looking at the airplane above.
Over a thousand ages
Each pilgrim steps in ancient tracks
Made new in that moment

Beyond the Field

My body tells me
things I may not yet admit:
There is trepidation in leaving home,
saying farewell to the familiar
I should be eating well
in preparation for the journey tomorrow
But my appetite has deserted me
I am unprepared
I feel so far away
I miss my loved ones

I wander the streets of the French village in the Pyrenees
It is early evening
The cobblestones
are laid in patterns of overlapping scallop shells
Symbol of the pilgrim journey
Reminder of our baptism
which was sufficient for my calling here
to this walled city
with the cold stone church
the tolling bells
the mass in French
the priests' blessing of les pèlerins
the stone arches that lead to bridges over the river
and then to the path over the mountains
One gate after another
A continual passing through
to the other side

Jeannine, the Basque host, welcomes me
Her simple preparation of a salad
the first of many blessings on the Camino
A different hunger has driven me
beyond the field
in search of the promise of Abraham
It is perhaps not a blind trust
But a willingness to walk only by
the light directly on the path in front of me
Seeing dimly, relying on unknown hands
that have passed the lantern
from one to another over the years
to show the way.
I pray that I will have the courage
to walk by that light
And to have the grace to carry it for another.

In the night
the snores of fellow pilgrims
reverberate in the small dormitory
Lying on my back, staring at the ceiling in the dark
I laugh out loud
I make my peace with the night
If I cannot sleep, I can rest
With or without sleep,
morning will come
and I will walk.
Later, in the night,
emboldened by some crazy courage
I pad across the room
and gently push against the snorer in the top bunk
until he shifts slightly
and the snoring stops
The room is quiet.
It is my first miracle on the Camino.

Passage

I am climbing for hours
Past Pyrenean villages
Whitewashed houses
Red tile roofs
A sign for fresh goat cheese
The air is chill beneath a blue sky,
bearing the faintest hint of spring
I am learning to look for the yellow arrows

The narrow fields of the valley
Are white with frost
like our breath in the morning air
Snow on the peaks we will cross
The hillsides fall below us as we climb
The earth still covered with the dry leaves of autumn
The fresh cold brook running past fields
pale green after receding snow
The branches of beech and hazel
bare but holding high the promise
that we will see spring before too long.
At mid-day we take the first of many siestas
Pilgrims sprawled on the leaves
with packs and boots scattered
in total surrender to the earth

In late afternoon, we cross the pass
The little village in France impossibly far behind
We have walked sixteen miles today.
Through the forest
we see the gray tiled roofs of Roncesvalles
We are in Spain
Bienvenidos peregrinos.

Passport stamps, sixteen bunks, showers, laundry
A simple meal with companions
A pilgrim mass sung in Spanish
The voices of the three priests
Blending and magnified
In the church from the middle ages
How many notes
have these old stone walls echoed,
How many blessings they have sheltered
It is evening of the first day.

Spring Melt

Leaving Roncesvalles, the Valley of Thorns
The sign says 790 kilometers to Santiago de Compostela
We take our pictures beside it
only half believing that we will actually walk there
We leave early before breakfast
and stop two miles away
for a warm omelette, a flaky croissant, strong coffee
Hemingway loved this country
Its trout streams, its wine, its passions
We cross the río Urrobi
It is March in these foothills
Snow on the peaks
We walk downhill
through forests and farms
Up through beech woods
Geese flying north overhead
Crows and blue tits in the branches.
We pass a white cross
where crones were burned as witches in the 1500s
Six centuries later, we still do not welcome them.
At lunch time,
we throw off our packs
Lying on the warm grass
we share oranges, cheese, bread, chocolate
We take off our boots
tend one another's blisters.

In the afternoon, we cross the río Erro,
and walk
Past barnyards
An old stone house
A new tractor
A courtyard with
a green bench holding red pots of geraniums
Two cats in the sun
under a plaster coat of arms
in an arched doorway

its thick door studded with wrought iron crosses
Windows above with wooden shutters
and lace curtains
Such a moveable feast of the senses
We can hardly carry it all,
Yet we take it with us
on the bridge over the Arga
The third river we have crossed today
Every moment flowing out of these old foothills
Full from bank to bank.

Across
the Bar

A flagstone path up through woods
to the next village
its fountain for pilgrims dated 1917
Pilgrims walked while war raged across the border
The meadows are greening
around a house built of red and gold stones
a grape vine trained against the sunny wall
Birds nest in the hedgerows near the purple anemones,
the white violets and blue forget-me-nots
As the full río Arga sings a song of spring alongside
We pause on the old arched bridge to listen to the music
A bag hangs from a front door knocker
holding the morning newspaper
and the day's fresh bread

This afternoon I walked with a Mexican through narrow alleys
in the city of the running of the bulls
Tonight I stay at a German albergue
Eat dinner with Americans and Canadians
Spanish dictionaries and maps
spread amidst the fresh salads and local red wine
Laughter spilling across the bar

North Atlantic Ocean

Santiago de Compostela

La Coruña

GALICIA

Lugo

Arca O Pino

Arzúa

Remonde

Morgade

Gonzar

Sarria

Samos

Triacastela

Vega de Valcarce

Pieros

Molinaseca

Foncebadón

Murias de Rechivaldo

Hospital de Órbigo

Villa de Mazarife

León

El Burgo Ranero

Sahagún

Mansilla de las Mulas

Hospital de la Condesa

Terradillos de los Templarios

Carrión de los Condes

Boadilla del Camino

Castrojeriz

Hornillos del Camino

Burgos

San Juan de Ortega

Tosantos

Santo Domingo de la Calzada

Grañón

Ventosa

Logroño

Torres del Río

Estella

Puente la Reina

Pamplona

Zubiri

Roncesvalles

St Jean Pied de Port

Bay of Biscay

FRANCE

NAVARRA

LA RIOJA

León

Palencia

Burgos

CASTILLA Y LEÓN

SPAIN

PORTUGAL

100 km

0   100 Miles

Alto de Perdón

I enter by the drawbridge which has welcomed pilgrims for millennia
Following the yellow arrows through winding streets
past brightly painted houses
and balconies hung with laundry
I stop at the covered market wandering from stall to stall
loading my pack with nuts, cheese, oranges, chocolate
to be savored on the day's walk
Leaving the city behind
I climb west,
Through red plowed fields ready for seed
Houses and churches rising up made of the same rich red earth
A great blue heron lifting gracefully from the stream.
I rest in one town in a dark bar
My pack on the floor
Stirring the hot chocolate thick as pudding
And stop again on a hillside bench for lunch.
In early afternoon, I slowly climb to the pass called Alto de Perdón
The Hill of Forgiveness
Metal silhouettes of pilgrims
On foot, horseback, burro, flank the pass
And face westward
Rusted like old joints
after centuries of wind and rain
The Camino endures.
On one ridge
A row of modern windmills whirrs, turning slowly
Two pilgrims from Italy and Mexico
Sit at the base of a stone monument
as one tends the bare feet of the other
Almond blossoms line the path as we descend
Cirrus clouds dancing like angels overhead.

On sore feet I detour two miles out of the way
To the round Knights Templar church at Eunate
When I arrive
I discover that it is closed on Mondays
This is Monday.
I trudge almost three miles more to Puente la Reina
to the monastery run by the Padres Reparadores
The dormitory is cold; I am tired.
Was it only this morning I was in Pamplona?

Chilled, I force myself to take a shower
do laundry in slow motion.
The irrepressible young Italian and the Mexican
go shopping for dinner
and bring back armloads to feed us all
Pasta, salad, wine
We cook and eat together
I sleep near the radiator
Buried in my sleeping bag with my hat on
And try to keep warm.

15

March 13 • Day 5
PUENTE LA REINA TO ESTELLA
13 MILES

Toda Felicidad

So far this has not been a journey of solitude.
I tell my companions that I need to walk alone
for a portion of each day.
I wait while one crosses the ancient Roman bridge
ahead of me until he is out of sight
Then I cross slowly enjoying the feel of my feet
on these old stones in the early morning light
Alone, I notice everything
The tall, dry golden rushes on the river bank
The thick oak doors fortified by iron crosses
The laundry drying on the line
against the stone wall
The tended park with its pilgrim fountain
and sculpture of the pilgrim's staff, hat and drinking gourd
The dirt path stretches out ahead
Winds up through pine forests
and down through vineyards
On the horizon is a hill town amidst red fields
Its buildings of ochre, sienna, and white
clustered together beneath the church;
I will walk to it.
A sheep stares at me
from the shadows of a hand-plastered barn
My feet are feeling the downhill pressure
of the old Roman roads
which wind up and over the next hill.
I rest against a tumbling stone wall
beneath gnarled olive trees
I marvel that I can simply walk
through a land of wine and olives under a blue sky.
I come to another water source built into a wall

surrounded by carvings of a star, a scallop shell,
a pilgrim's staff and gourd.
These words are cut into the stone:

> "Buen pan
> Excelente agua
> Y vino, carne y
> Pescado, llena de
> toda felicidad."

The afternoon is very warm
Walking up a hot hill
A yellow butterfly dances before me
shows me the way

A breeze to fan me, gracias a Dios
What I need is provided when I need it

I cross four rivers
In the evening, in Estella on the river
Pilgrims from five countries
Tell stories over food and wine
The priest at the mass
blesses each one of us in our own language.
Toda Felicidad

North Atlantic Ocean

Santiago de Compostela

FRANCE

Bay of Biscay

St Jean Pied de Port

Roncesvalles

Santo Domingo de la Calzada

Pamplona

Puente la Reina

Estella

Zubiri

La Coruña

Arca O Pino

Arzúa

Remonde

Morgade

Gonzar

Samos

Sarria

Triacastela

Pieros

Molinaseca

Foncebadón

Vega de Valcarce

Hospital de la Condesa

Murias de Rechivaldo

Hospital de Órbigo

Villar de Mazarife

León

El Burgo Ranero

Terradillos de los Templarios

Carrión de los Condes

Boadilla del Camino

Castrojeriz

Hornillos del Camino

San Juan de Ortega

Burgos

Tosantos

Torres del Río

Logroño

Ventosa

Grañón

Mansilla de las Mulas

GALICIA

Lugo

León

Palencia

Burgos

NAVARRA

LA RIOJA

100 km

0

100 Miles

CASTILLA Y LEÓN

SPAIN

PORTUGAL

March 14 • Day 6
Estella to Torres del Río
18 miles

Learnings

Today I walked too far
Past the Irache pilgrim fountain
fabled to have free wine;
The fountain was dry.
Eighteen miles, and my feet complain
I did not like the hostel at the first town
So I walked five miles more on a hot afternoon.
It was too much
I did not come to the Camino to rush
I am learning to listen to my body.
At the hostel,
the shower is either scalding or freezing
Yet the day had its own simple blessings
A croissant
A breeze
The smell of almond trees
The tended gardens
The wine and conversation at dinner
and a fellow pilgrim who gives me
a tube of Vaseline for my blistered feet.
I am learning to be.

In the evening
I meet a man who has walked 97,000 kilometers
to different sanctuaries in the world
He tells his stories
I am too tired to write in my journal
I am learning to listen.

North Atlantic Ocean

Santiago de Compostela

La Coruña

Arca O Pino

Arzúa

Remonde

Morgade

Gonzar

Samos

Sarría

Triacastela

Pieros

Vega de Valcarce

Molinaseca

Foncebadón

Hospital de la Condesa

Murias de Rechivaldo

Hospital de Órbigo

Villar de Mazarife

León

El Burgo Ranero

Sahagún

Terradillos de los Templarios

Carrión de los Condes

Boadilla del Camino

Castrojeriz

Hornillos del Camino

Burgos

San Juan de Ortega

Tosantos

Santo Domingo de la Calzada

Grañón

Ventosa

Logroño

Torres del Río

Estella

Puente la Reina

Pamplona

Zubiri

Roncesvalles

St Jean Pied de Port

Bay of Biscay

GALICIA

Lugo

Mansilla de las Mulas

León

Palencia

Burgos

NAVARRA

LA RIOJA

F R A N C E

100 km

0   100 Miles

CASTILLA Y LEÓN

S P A I N

PORTUGAL

Santa María

Steep path down through vineyards and olive groves
Curved stone huts are shade for the farmers.
Around a bend,
an unexpected bush of rosemary
fragrant purple blossoms buzzing with bees.
At mid-day I buy 40 Euros worth of band-aids
Eat lunch in the shade of the cathedral
Smile at an old man talking to a sparrow.
Another six miles to the city of Logroño;
I have walked 100 miles in seven days
I will stay tonight with the sister of a friend.
I learn again about hospitality
From a woman who lives the compassion of her namesake,
Santa María
A warm embrace
A clean room
A shower with fresh towels
A salad of garlic, anchovies, red peppers, olives
A plate of potato and octopus
A deep sleep without the sound of snoring
Awakening to smoothly folded laundry
Fresh squeezed orange juice
Muesli and green tea
A bag of nuts and raisins for the trail
A warm farewell.
May I also welcome pilgrims
with such simple generosities as these.

March 16 • Day 8
LOGROÑO TO VENTOSA
13 MILES

La Rioja

I am in the country of red wine,
La Rioja
Even the streets in Logroño are paved
with red tiles of grape clusters and leaves
A mural traces the Camino through wine country
In its corner, a scallop shell
painted against the rays of the sun, and these words:
"Nunca caminarás solo" – "you'll never walk alone"
A stork watches as I pass beneath the iglesia
with its carvings of scallop shells, symbols of baptism
And its statue of Santiago Matamoros,
St. James the Moorslayer;
we are complex human beings.

Resting on a bench
A pilgrim from Holland tells me
to carry a whole raw carrot in my pocket
The chewing will sustain me over a long day
I stop at a lakeside café, drink a café con leche
My feet up on a chair
I gaze at the lake
I am learning to rest.
I walk over gently rolling hills
red earth planted in vineyards
Each almond tree in blossom a new blessing
I pass a fence protecting peregrinos
from the national highway below
the wires entwined with crosses
Made of twigs, of straw, of paper
Fashioned by the hands of pilgrims
who have left their prayers along the road.

This is also the country of the bulls
It is said they are raised in a short, happy life
before they run through the streets of Pamplona
to face the matadors
A huge silhouette of a bull
dominates the skyline
above the red earth, the red-tiled roofs.
The day is cool, overcast
I buy some bread, cheese, an apple
Sit huddled with other pilgrims
on the cold stone steps
of the town square at mid-day
In the afternoon
I walk with the woman from Holland

We get lost at a crossroads
and go several miles off route to another village
In taking a wrong turn, we find along the way
that our children are the same age,
and we pass another beautiful tree in blossom.
San Saturnino in Ventosa
provides a warm haven for pilgrims
A long table and a fireplace
A place to do laundry
A small shop for groceries
Bottles of wine with the albergue's own label
We cook pasta and enjoy the wine, the company
Pilgrims from Iceland, Canada, Holland, Germany,
and the United States
Complete, I go to bed early.

North Atlantic Ocean

Bay of Biscay

FRANCE

Santiago de Compostela
Arca O Pino
Arzúa
Remonde
Morgade
Gonzar
Samos
Triacastela
Sarria
Hospital de la Condesa
Molinaseca
Foncebadón
Pieros
Vega de Valcarce
Murias de Rechivaldo
Hospital de Órbigo
Villar de Mazarife
León
El Burgo Ranero
Sahagún
Terradillos de los Templarios
Carrión de los Condes
Boadilla del Camino
Castrojeriz
Hornillos del Camino
Burgos
San Juan de Ortega
Tosantos
Santo Domingo de la Calzada
Grañón
Ventosa
Logroño
Torres del Río
Estella
Puente la Reina
Pamplona
Zubiri
Roncesvalles
St Jean Pied de Port
Mansilla de las Mulas

La Coruña
GALICIA
Lugo
León
Palencia
Burgos
NAVARRA
LA RIOJA
CASTILLA Y LEÓN
SPAIN
PORTUGAL

100 km
0   100 Miles

March 17 • Day 9
Ventosa to Santo Domingo de la Calzada
19 miles

Eso Es

The morning is soft with spring
An almond tree in bloom
overhangs the stony track
that winds past freshly plowed hills and green fields
The still-wintering grape vines are black stumps
in gnarled rows along the red earth
I am walking towards the mountains in the far distance
their peaks white with snow
Someone has made a cairn next to the road
Stones piled on one another
honoring the journey
as each pilgrim walks by.
The March air is fresh and raw
I pass a barn painted with the sign,
"Eso es Navarre"
I wave to the farmer
tell him his land is beautiful. He grins.
On the edge of town
Storks pick their way through the newly turned earth
The dormitory that evening sleeps more than forty
The long table is piled with plates of spaghetti
Chunks of bread, bottles of wine and water
We speak French, German, English, Dutch
From the second story
I watch the clouds turn pink over red-tiled roofs

Refuge

By now, the ancient cobblestones seem familiar
The narrow streets, the old stone churches
The stork nests of sticks on the towers.
In the field, the hay bales rise
stacked in rectangles tall as houses
The wind is strong and cold from the west
I struggle uphill against it
wearing all of my layers.
Too tired to continue,
I stumble into the old stone church
Hospital de Peregrinos San Juan Bautista
Sheltering pilgrims
for eight hundred years.

The thick wooden door stands open in welcome
its iron knocker hammered in the shape
of a scallop shell, walking staff, and gourd
the March sunlight warming the floor of the entry
The stone stairway winds upward
Halfway to the second floor there is a window ledge
with a sign in many languages: here is where we are to leave
our "botas, carpari, shoes, chaussures, schine, cipo…"
The volunteers welcome me with open hands
warm sweet rice, hot coffee
The wood stove radiates heat
I spend the afternoon in the loft,
warm in my sleeping bag, resting, napping,
Lulled by the soft strains of guitar
And the murmur of voices below

North Atlantic Ocean
Bay of Biscay

Santiago de Compostela
Arca O Pino
Arzúa
Remonde
Morgade
Gonzar
Samos
Triacastela
Hospital de la Condesa
Vega de Valcarce
Molinaseca
Foncebadón
Murias de Rechivaldo
Hospital de Órbigo
Villar de Mazarife
León
El Burgo Ranero
Sahagún
Terradillos de los Templarios
Carrión de los Condes
Boadilla del Camino
Castrojeriz
Hornillos del Camino
Burgos
San Juan de Ortega
Tosantos
Santo Domingo de la Calzada
Grañón
Ventosa
Logroño
Torres del Río
Estella
Puente la Reina
Pamplona
Zubiri
Roncesvalles
St Jean Pied de Port
FRANCE

La Coruña
GALICIA
Lugo

León
Mansilla de las Mulas
Palencia
Burgos
NAVARRA
LA RIOJA

100 km
0   100 Miles

SPAIN

CASTILLA Y LEÓN

PORTUGAL

March 19 • Day 11
GRAÑÓN TO TOSANTOS
13 MILES

No Hay Calor

The lion of March
is at play today
mixing up wind, clouds, sun
It is raw and cold
I stop in a sheltered town square
On a bench in the sun,
I take off my boots
Peel an orange
Feed some cheese to a hungry cat
The albergue in the town
  Is still closed for the winter
 I walk on in wind and mist
  In the evening, I stop
  at the only place open in the next town
   There is no heat except for a radiator in the kitchen
   I sit and have a cup of tea with the volunteers
   They bring a portable space heater
   to briefly heat the room before bed
   Just as it takes the edge off the cold
   they take it away again
  We sleep on mats on the floor
  Under cold wool blankets
  I wait for the morning
   and to be walking again
    At least the walking will keep me warm.

North Atlantic Ocean

Santiago de Compostela
La Coruña
Arca O Pino
Arzúa
Remonde
Hospital de la Condesa
Morgade
Gonzar
Samos
Sarría
Triacastela
Lugo
GALICIA
Molinaseca
Foncebadón
Murias de Rechivaldo
Hospital de Órbigo
Vega de Valcarce
Pieros
Villar de Mazarife
León
El Burgo Ranero
Terradillos de los Templarios
Sahagún
Mansilla de las Mulas
León
Carrión de los Condes
Boadilla del Camino
Palencia
Castrojeriz
Hornillos del Camino
Burgos
Burgos
San Juan de Ortega
Tosantos
Santo Domingo de la Calzada
Grañón
Ventosa
Logroño
Torres del Río
Estella
Puente la Reina
Pamplona
Zubiri
Bay of Biscay
St Jean Pied de Port
Roncesvalles
FRANCE
NAVARRA
LA RIOJA

SPAIN

CASTILLA Y LEÓN

100 km
0   100 Miles

PORTUGAL

29

March 20 • Day 12
TOSANTOS TO SAN JUAN DE ORTEGA
12 MILES

Light and Warmth

Another cold day
periods of sun that light
but do not heat
I walk through fields
Then along a busy highway
The trucks rattle by, very close
I am unsettled to be near traffic and speed
after days of walking in rural peace
In late morning I seek out a place to get warm
and happen upon a quiet hotel
Its bar is sunlit, the chairs padded
The walls stuccoed a soft pink
I take off my pack
and lean it carefully against the wall
I order a cup of tea and a sweet roll.
The waitress is newly arrived from Romania
She sees that I am a pilgrim
Instead of a cup, she brings me a pot of tea
and a whole basket of assorted breads
"Eat what you can and take the rest for later," she insists.
I do not know her name
I wish I could tell her now
That she is forever in my memory
As a light of hospitality on the Camino.
Warmed through, I start out again
This time steeply uphill through snow flurries.
At the top of a rise I find two friends from Holland and Germany
waiting for me in a cold shelter at the side of the trail
Excited to see me, they wave
Many times it is the little gestures
that welcome and include.

Passing the hilltop monument to the Civil War of 1936
we rest later on in a forest
pool our resources for lunch
Cookies, apples, oranges, sausage, cheese, chips, chocolate
We stop for the evening in a 15th Century nunnery
Again there is no heat
I do my laundry in cold water
and hang it on the balcony clothesline
hoping it will dry and not freeze
We find heat next door in the bar
linger there the rest of the evening
writing in our journals
ordering omelettes for dinner and
one hot chocolate after another
just to stay in a warm place

North Atlantic Ocean

Santiago de Compostela
La Coruña
Arca O Pino
Arzúa
Remonde
Morgade
Gonzar
Sarria
Samos
Triacastela
Hospital de la Condesa
Vega de Valcarce
Molinaseca
Foncebadón
Murias de Rechivaldo
Hospital de Órbigo
Villar de Mazarife
León
Piedros
El Burgo Ranero
Mansilla de las Mulas
Terradillos de los Templarios
Carrión de los Condes
Sahagún
Boadilla del Camino
Castrojeriz
Hornillos del Camino
Burgos
San Juan de Ortega
Tosantos
Santo Domingo de la Calzada
Grañón
Ventosa
Logroño
Torres del Río
Estella
Puente la Reina
Pamplona
Zubiri
Roncesvalles
St Jean Pied de Port

Bay of Biscay

FRANCE

GALICIA
Lugo
León
Palencia
Burgos
NAVARRA
LA RIOJA

SPAIN

CASTILLA Y LEÓN

PORTUGAL

100 km
0   100 Miles

March 21 • Day 13
SAN JUAN DE ORTEGA TO BURGOS
16 MILES

Yielding

This morning I am walking in sleet and hail
It is gray and cold and Burgos is 16 miles away
I go up and over a hill
There is a stone labyrinth on top
I would like to walk it, but it is cold
and I have 15 miles to go
I meet up with friends in a nearby town
We huddle near a heater, drink coffee
eat most of our food.
We decide to take the rural path to Burgos
But the sleet has turned the clay to mud
that clings to our boots
until each foot weighs several pounds more
We retreat and walk by the roads
Passing the Burgos airport
and then onto the concrete sidewalks of this large city
I see a highway sign
"Ud, no tiene la prioridad"
"you do not have the right of way"
I decide that yielding
might be an ongoing theme of my pilgrimage
embracing what is in the present moment.
My European friends want to stop at a Burger King
A Burger King in Burgos,
A city famous for its tapas
We are modern pilgrims indeed.
The albergue, run by the City, has many floors
On the first floor, the boot lockers pull out
higher than our heads
each storing at least twenty pairs of boots
There is room here for hundreds of pilgrims

Amigos del
Camino de Santiago
Burgos

2 1 MAR 2012

Three of us share a washer and dryer
Do a large load of laundry
Prepare a meal together
Take hot showers
The bunk beds have electrical outlets
for our phone chargers
We are warm!
But it is a large city
I am anxious to be back in the Spanish countryside.

March 22 • Day 14
BURGOS TO HORNILLOS DEL CAMINO
13 MILES

El Camino Me Hace a Mí

The golden spires
Of the 13th century Catedral de Santa María
glow with early light
bless us from above
as we walk through their long shadows
in the cold morning air
on cobblestones trod by millions of pilgrim feet.
We stop at a panadería for fresh-baked baguettes
On a cold stone bench on the outskirts of the city
Three peregrinos break the night's fast
Bread, jam, sausage, mandarin orange
We walk on, up onto the Meseta
Exposed to the wide open expanse of sky
The gently undulating furrowed earth
with new green blades of wheat
surely growing toward the sun
The weeping willow bends over a stream
Sunning its yellow green tendrils
The air today is more softly raw
I am walking into spring.

I stop for coffee in a bar
The dark walls sport animal trophies
and there is a hunting show on the television
I pass an old shepherd herding his flock into a field
The road is a ribbon of chalk
leading up into the hills under soft clouds
I realize I am carrying food and water
that I don't stop to eat and drink
I am learning to carry things only as long as they are useful
And to trust that what I need
will be on the road ahead

I meet companions at a roadside park
We take off our boots, laugh
Spread out our loaves and fishes
Make a meal
I rest for the evening in Hornillos del Camino
The narrow street of the old stone town
is lined with thick doors wide-planked
opening onto now empty houses and sheepfolds
Around the table, we share olives, cheese,
Sausage, bread, pasta, oranges, mint tea.
A poster in the refuge reads
"No hago yo el Camino, el Camino me hace a mí."
"I don't make the Camino, the Camino makes me."

March 23 • Day 15
HORNILLOS DEL CAMINO TO CASTROJERIZ
13 MILES

Manna

I am walking a dirt track
on the wide Meseta
Fields on both sides of me
Spring clouds high above
The day is glorious and
My feet hurt.
After six miles
I stop in the sun
in the stone courtyard of a bar
where other pilgrims are also gathered
I order a café con leche
and two muffins
then a potato omelette
I take a picture of my bare feet
Three bandages on my toes
One toenail purple
They rest propped up on the iron table
next to a tube of foot ointment,
my guidebook, and the glass cup of coffee.
I have what I need for this day.

I walk on to the old convent of San Antón
A sundial carved in the wall
tells the hours of the centuries
where monks healed the sick
under the sign of the Tau
and left bread for pilgrims in the stone nichos.
Under the archway carved with saints,
I write a prayer for a future pilgrim
and leave it in the nicho
Bread for their journey.

North Atlantic Ocean

Santiago de Compostela
La Coruña
Arca O Pino
Arzúa
Remonde
Morgade
Gonzar
Samos
Sarria
Triacastela
Hospital de la Condesa
Murias de Rechivaldo
Molinaseca
Foncebadón
Pieros
Vega de Valcarce
Hospital de Órbigo
Villar de Mazarife
León
El Burgo Ranero
Sahagún
Terradillos de los Templarios
Carrión de los Condes
Boadilla del Camino
Castrojeriz
Hornillos del Camino
Burgos
San Juan de Ortega
Tosantos
Santo Domingo de la Calzada
Grañón
Ventosa
Logroño
Torres del Río
Estella
Puente la Reina
Pamplona
Zubiri
Roncesvalles
St Jean Pied de Port

Bay of Biscay

FRANCE

GALICIA

Lugo

Triacastela

Mansilla de las Mulas

León

Palencia

Burgos

LA RIOJA

NAVARRA

100 km

0   100 Miles

CASTILLA Y LEÓN

S P A I N

PORTUGAL

March 24 • Day 16
CASTROJERIZ TO BOADILLA DEL CAMINO
12 MILES

Moments

Today there is no hurry
The road stretches out before me
and I walk it
The rushes along the canals
glow like tapers in the early morning light
A young woman
hobbles slowly behind me
I wait for her
Ask about her limp
Give her the knee brace from my pack
that I have carried for such a moment.
I do not need it
and if I do, I will find one

The day unfurls around me
River flowing under a stone bridge
A bus of weekend pilgrim families
walking this stretch, too
I find myself judging their light-hearted outing
Can there be one "right" way to make a pilgrimage?
I bless them in providing another chance
For my own healing

On the horizon
At the top of a hill
A grove of pine trees beckons
I stop there, grateful for the shade and the view
I sketch the hill
and the road I have traveled this day
The pencils reflect the colors of spring earth and sky

At night, Begoña and her family
at Boadilla del Camino welcome pilgrims
With green grass, laundry, a full-course meal
Garlic soup; fish; salad; ice cream; wine
My dinner companions are from France, Japan;
We toast one another
The Frenchman and his wife
have walked the Camino before;
They are starting a charity
Donkey carts that will allow those unable to walk
to make the pilgrimage to Santiago
His memories of the Camino are of joy and happiness
He will not know it
But his words and his joy stay with me
Will bless me in the difficult days to come.

March 25 • Day 17
BOADILLA DEL CAMINO TO CARRIÓN DE LOS CONDES
16 MILES

Ready Grace

Today my heart is laid open
Not by choice, but by grace
I walk 16 miles
Alone in body and thoughts
The day is hot
I trudge uphill in the afternoon sun
My spirit trudges, too
I am headed for Carrión de los Condes
And the Albergue Santa María
The last three miles are challenging
I find myself saying
"I need the ministry of nuns."
God knows I am ready
and lays open my heart.
I see that my generosity is conditional
I am afraid of losing things
I live as if there will not be enough.
That evening, in the shelter of the nuns
I am rejected by another pilgrim
And deep sobs rise up and pour forth
I am inconsolable
God, I say,
I asked you to open my heart
But could you do it more comfortably?
The nuns in their simple habits sing to us
the ancient songs of the Camino
The tears continue to overflow,
A great deep well springing up
The nuns embrace me
Pat my back
Say, "pobrecita, mucha anima"

They give me a laminated card of their saint
María Auxiliadora, Mary the Helper,
And a room by myself
I surrender the sorrow
I trust that God
Will use it for healing.
Under a plain wooden cross
hung with a scallop shell
I sleep.

March 26 • Day 18
CARRIÓN DE LOS CONDES TO TERRADILLOS DE LOS TEMPLARIOS
17 MILES

Balm

Balm comes in many forms this day
The bright stars overhead as I leave before dawn
The glimmer of flowing waters at first light
My shadow before me leading to the horizon
There is nothing to separate me from my thoughts
and my feet on the path
No café for ten miles, no breakfast, no coffee
No interruptions for God's healing
I walk, fasting, and I meditate
The sorrows of the day before
are bathed in the new morning light
I cross eight streams, our courses overrunning
The geese return to the north
Two hawks soar
An older man tips his hat
To the beautiful young lady
He is referring to me
My spirit rises as peace descends.
This day marks the halfway point on my journey
And I see how far I have to go
I think how little I understand
about unconditional love and grace
The irony of living out of scarcity
in the presence of unending abundance
In the mid-afternoon I stop
The albergue has a garden
I write, wash clothes
I sit in a nearby park
listen to the steady sound
of a bee buzzing nearby

It turns out to be an old dog
snoring in the sunny courtyard
I am grateful
The music and words of a Gaelic blessing song come to me
"Deep peace of the running wave to you…."
Where there is wounding
there is also consolation
And balm comes in many forms

March 27 • Day 19
TERRADILLOS DE LOS TEMPLARIOS TO SAHAGÚN
8 MILES

Mud and Straw

My shadow points west down the dirt track
All around me ground and sky
The morning light on the deep furrow
of newly turned earth
Weaving rich patterns of promise
The footprint in the dust ahead of me
bears the press of crosses from its sole
The hillside of the town in the distance
filled with cool dark caves
where wine was stored in days of old.
In a little shop run by a German couple
Surrounded by Easter decorations
I am surprised to see
my pilgrim friend
Two days ago we caused each other pain
and we have not seen each other since
We sit inside in the warm sun
Give and receive a small healing
Not so much in words as in the invitation
To drink strong coffee, her treat,
Eat yogurt with honey and almonds
Try the good chocolate.
I walk on later
The ditches are running
The garlic plants already knee-high
I pass a stone barn
Despite, or perhaps to bless, its ordinary function
Someone has taken the care
To press into the earth walls
A wooden cross
A row of large scallop shells

A border of smaller shells
Mud and straw mixed and patted by hand.
All day I am surrounded as I walk
By ancient buildings and paths
Old stone bridges
under newly budding trees
A chapel courtyard entry intricately paved
with small, interlocking stones
in the shape of a heart
Shadows and light, past and future,
Pain and hope, dust to dust
I am full
With chances in each moment
To hold it all

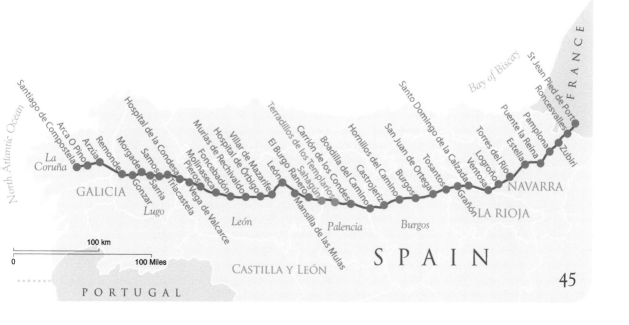

Lark Song

In the early morning
I step into the little shop
Say goodbye to the grocer
who was kind to me yesterday
as I bought bread and chocolate
"Buen Camino!" we smile and wave
I cross the old Roman bridge out of town
My shadow is long on the path ahead
The hand-painted sign
"Santiago 315 km Ultreia"
Its yellow arrow points west
Another day of balm
Pear trees bloom outside an old chapel
The ravens waddle in greening fields
making me smile
Waterfowl swim in the wetlands
The farmer drives his flock of sheep through the town
And the storks make their nest on the church steeple.
High above me
The larks sing for free
Their notes falling around me
An extravagant shower of blessings from the sky
Drenching me in abundant joy.

North Atlantic Ocean

Santiago de Compostela

La Coruña

Arca O Pino

Arzúa

Remonde

Morgade

Gonzar

Samos

Sarria

Hospital de la Condesa

Triacastela

Vega de Valcarce

Molinaseca

Fonçebadón

Pieros

Murias de Rechivaldo

Hospital de Órbigo

Villar de Mazarife

León

Mansilla de las Mulas

El Burgo Ranero

Sahagún

Terradillos de los Templarios

Carrión de los Condes

Boadilla del Camino

Castrojeriz

Hornillos del Camino

Burgos

San Juan de Ortega

Tosantos

Santo Domingo de la Calzada

Grañón

Ventosa

Logroño

Torres del Río

Estella

Puente la Reina

Pamplona

Zubiri

Roncesvalles

St Jean Pied de Port

Bay of Biscay

FRANCE

NAVARRA

LA RIOJA

GALICIA

Lugo

León

Palencia

Burgos

CASTILLA Y LEÓN

SPAIN

PORTUGAL

100 km

0   100 Miles

The Pure Joy of Orange

I leave before sunrise
Lavender dawn lighting the dirt track
and reflecting upwards from the full ditches
Water bubbling its way into the field
Reeds glowing at their tips like candles
A smiling bearded man in a French beret
serves me coffee at a bar
The art and language of many pilgrims cover the wall
Exuberant peregrino graffiti
A mother and daughter from Spain and France
reunite every year to walk this week together
I take a picture of them wearing orange socks
and eating fresh oranges;
We laugh at the pure joy of orange
under a blue sky.

At the Amigos del Peregrino
Laura welcomes all the pilgrims
She has been there for 14 years
creating a home on the road
The courtyard walls are painted yellow
Pilgrim laundry strung between the flowerpots
Scallop shells hang from the ceiling,
mobiles of blessings overhead.
Signs welcome in four languages:
"Manger, essen, come, eat"
Pilgrims place their small flag pins
On the world map on the wall
Showing their home countries
too numerous to count
That night we cook together
France, Holland, Switzerland, United States

We toast to my son, who turns 23 today
I fall asleep in the bedroom dormitory
A community of the world.

Reunion

I take a picture of myself and my backpack
My shadow long against a building in the early light
My nose red beneath my wool cap in the morning cold
I pass a bird's nest in a young tree
If the birds were not singing
my heart would still sing
I am walking to meet my peregrina daughter
And she is traveling to meet me
at an inn at the end of today's trail
But that is twelve miles away, and until then
I walk, one foot ahead of the other
I stop twice to rest
First a just-baked croissant and coffee
at a bakery owned by a young woman
She has courage on her own camino.
In another town
after a long trudge uphill in hot sun
the Torre Bar owner
makes me a fresh potato tortilla
adds a slice of cake for free
I walk the last two miles on hard pavement through León
I am here! She is coming tonight!
My dear husband
Has reserved one night for us
At the famed Parador hotel
I check in; take a picture of my pack and walking stick
leaning against the lobby desk
Seemingly out of place
in sumptuous surroundings
And yet very much at home
in this 12th century pilgrim hospital

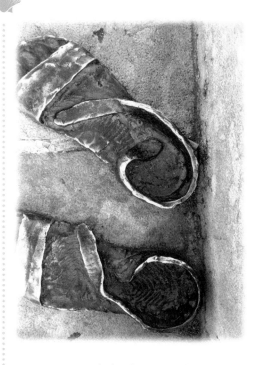

How many pilgrim feet
have crossed this threshold over the centuries,
been refreshed and healed here?
Our room overlooks the treetops
And the río Bernesga
The afternoon lulls me with its green shade
the faraway sounds of traffic and water
murmured voices from the plaza below
Rest is deep.

Later, I walk to the cathedral
With its beautiful stained glass windows
At 7:15 p.m., Laura's bus arrives
What a joy to see her as she steps off
Back on the Camino where she was a peregrina
five years ago in this same month
Her hair is in two long braids as it was then,
She wears a skirt, leggings, hiking boots
Her smile is as wide as mine
We link arms, talk happily
all the way to the hotel

Later we eat a light dinner at the bar
A salad and a sandwich of egg, salmon, asparagus
Fruit and sherbet, a glass of wine
Returning to our room
We laugh to find my long underwear, my "pajamas,"
laid out on the bed for our evening rest
along with Parador shell-shaped chocolates
We know we are blessed
to be walking this road together
Mother and daughter peregrinas
We sleep well in the cool, clean sheets.

Feast

Deep sleep gives way slowly
Light filtering through open shutters
A gentle breeze carrying the
chatter of magpies, the song of blackbirds
the rooster's call.
Surrounded by vacationing families
we wear our pilgrim clothing
into the Parador dining room
Enjoy a leisurely breakfast from the abundant buffet
We laugh with delight
and do not apologize
We are going to enjoy every crumb of croissant
multiple cups of tea
the fresh fruits, cheese, breads, jam
There have not been too many pilgrim breakfasts
like this on the Camino
We stop at the lovely arched cloisters
The courtyard set with intricate patterns
of small river stones
We are reminded daily that
we are walking the same path of the earliest pilgrims
more than one thousand years later
And we marvel at the space of one life
In this millennium of lifetimes
Every day with a daughter is a miracle
It is hard to express the joy
captured in a picture
our two faces pressed together
under ancient arches
feet on timeworn stones

We walk out of the city into farmland
passing bodegas with wine
aging in their cool hidden interiors
The daffodils grow in hedgerows
next to newly plowed fields,
old plank doors in faded green
We climb up a long hill
into high open bush country
mountains in the distance
We eat Laura's "Paddington" energy bars
made with the things Paddington liked to eat
Stop to watch a mass of wriggling caterpillars
crossing the dirt track on their own migration

We walk for a while
with a young man from South Africa
That night we stay
at the Albergue San Antonio de Pádua
The gourmet chef gives us a room of our own
Calls us to a dinner of arugula salad
Pumpkin soup, pasta, wine
Banana and chocolate crepes for dessert
We invite Kerrie,
a young actress from Ireland, to join us
It has been a day full of pure happiness
From start to finish

Domingo de Ramos

We choose an unhurried pace on this Palm Sunday,
Domingo de Ramos
We sleep late, linger over toast and tea
Then walk past fields
being irrigated for the first time this spring
Snow melting on the mountain peaks in the distance
We wave to the farmers in their waders
shin deep in the furrows
And to a young man high up in his tractor
looking happy to be out in sowing time
We spend a long lunch hour
sitting on the edge of an acequia
listening to its musical song rise and fall
Realizing how nurturing is the sound of water
erasing any weariness in the day
The blackbirds, ravens, magpies
are enjoying the soft sunshine
We pass through a little village
People are holding their laurel branches
waiting for the procession to begin
We rest over café con leche in a little bar

The Albergue San Miguel in Hospital de Órbigo
welcomes us with open arms and a glass of wine
The hospitaler, Alberto, shares with us his good beef stew
Later, we sketch the ancient Camino bridge
knowing that countless pilgrims have walked over its arches
We make our dinner, invite a Dutch couple
and a man from Spain to break bread with us
We laugh as we fall asleep
next to the snoring cave bear in the next bed.

Solace

My daughter leaves on the morning bus
and again I walk alone, missing her
The land soothes me
Red fields, green wheat
Oak woods, pine forest
Farmers irrigating their fields
Churches with their stork nests.
Later there will be rain,
so today I walk farther.
In the gathering clouds
I arrive at the albergue
one half hour before the rain and hail
Again, I have had what I needed
And a rainbow shines in the distance after the storm
I eat dinner with a woman from Slovakia
A man from Korea and
eight Irish ladies who walk one week each year
Tomorrow the road heads up into the mountains.

North Atlantic Ocean

Santiago de Compostela

La Coruña

Arca O Pino

Arzúa

Remonde

Morgade

Gonzar

Samos

Sarría

Triacastela

Hospital de la Condesa

Vega de Valcarce

Pieros

Molinaseca

Foncebadón

Murias de Rechivaldo

Hospital de Órbigo

Villar de Mazarife

León

Mansilla de las Mulas

El Burgo Ranero

Sahagún

Terradillos de los Templarios

Carrión de los Condes

Boadilla del Camino

Castrojeriz

Hornillos del Camino

Burgos

San Juan de Ortega

Tosantos

Santo Domingo de la Calzada

Grañón

Ventosa

Logroño

Torres del Río

Estella

Puente la Reina

Pamplona

Zubiri

Roncesvalles

St Jean Pied de Port

Bay of Biscay

GALICIA

Lugo

León

Palencia

Burgos

CASTILLA Y LEÓN

NAVARRA

LA RIOJA

SPAIN

FRANCE

PORTUGAL

100 km

0

100 Miles

Everywhere the Dance

The April morning is cool, overcast
The dirt track leads upward
The clouds are gray
But everywhere there are signs
of people who celebrate life
They have planted young fruit trees along the path
intentional blessings of white apple blossoms
An arrow in the road made of stones
A rainbow painted underneath the scallop shells
on the old stile
Yellow gorse blooms in the red earth
In a village made of the same red stone
someone has built the wall
around an oak tree
Setting a bench for rest
under its branches
How many pilgrims since
have sat in its shade?
In a cowboy bar
I stop for coffee, chocolate, egg and potato tortilla
The owner has never been to cowboy country
but his bar is lined with hats and stirrups
The road rises up toward the range of mountains
A flock of sheep crosses the path
guarded by a huge sheep dog
As I climb, I pass crosses
Woven into wire fences
framed by blooms of purple heather
I arrive at Foncebadón
Rumored home of wild dogs

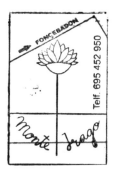

Instead I find horses, chickens,
A roaring fire and massages for a small donation
Who can resist?
Rows of boots
The unexpected joyful reunion
with pilgrims from two weeks past
Our host makes paella for everyone
Then brings out his drum

The Austrian plays his guitar
The Irish women sing
Thirty pilgrims link arms, dance
Then lie in sleeping bags in rows in the attic
quiet songs in the dark
Tired, full, slipping into slumber that restores.

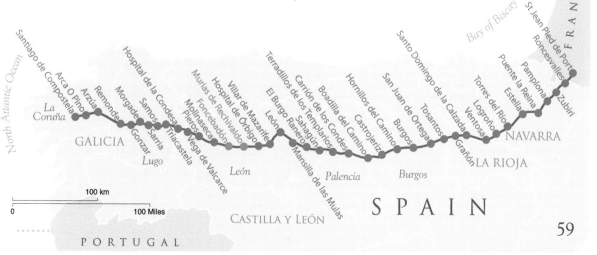

FONCEBADÓN TO MOLINASECA
13 MILES

Crossroads

I step out of the albergue into the fog
The path vanishes beyond the houses
At the fork of a dirt road, in the mist,
There is a cross
Its location says: "choose;" it reminds me
that we are always choosing in each moment
It is the perfect symbol
of the walk to the Cruz de Ferro
The iron cross on the high mountain pass
Where thousands of pilgrims
have brought their broken dreams
left a stone they have carried
We can only see what is before us
We carry only what we need
We leave behind what no longer serves

I walk in the muffled quiet alone between groups
I savor the cool air, the time to listen to my heart
Tall pines rise out of the mist above the heather
Witnesses of the journey.
I feel fortunate to arrive alone at the iron cross
Climbing up the pile of stones
I lay my hand on the wooden pole
Surrounded by the offerings of others
symbols of their burdens, griefs, joys
handwritten notes, photos of children, stones
I place a red rock
in memory of my home in New Mexico
I ask to let go of any grief

Sense of scarcity or lack, of past hurts
In a wedge of the cross I leave
A white, heart-shaped rock,
Sign of my hopes
to be more generous, trusting
To love and give without conditions
To live in the present.

Leaving the cross,
I continue all day in the rain, reflecting
Up hill and down.
Everywhere, signs of new life in the fog
Heather purple in snow
A water trough for cattle
Stone streets shining with rain
Trees with spring blossoms
And a hand-painted sign looming out of the mist:
"Dios es Amor"—God is Love.

Smoothed by Hand

Today the little things:
The flowering orchards on both sides of me
Kindness pouring from the hearts of strangers
Ducking out of the rain
into a bar with opera music playing
Omelette with sliced tomatoes on the side
and tea with hot milk.
Walking a while with an Austrian,
a man on the street stops us
tells us to wait a moment
returns with handfuls of walnuts from his tree
"Buen Camino," he says.
Losing our way,
a young woman drives us back
to the correct path
Getting at last to a village
to find the albergue closed,
someone treats me to a glass of wine
before we walk on
Another turns back,
slips her arm through mine
when I lag behind
Tears of exhaustion and gratitude flow
That evening, the hospitalera sings a Basque song
as we eat a hearty meal
Vegetable couscous, thick slabs of crusty bread
Share wine from a carafe

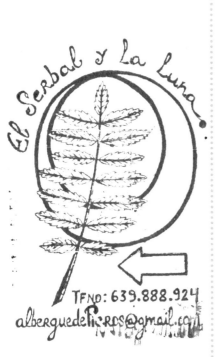

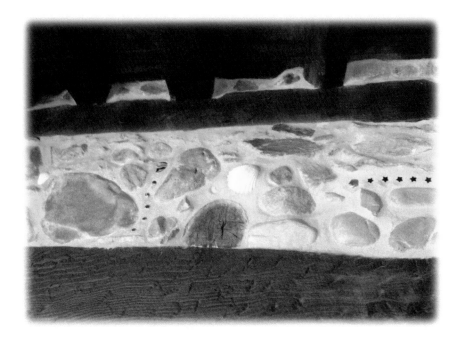

Sing together to the music of a guitar
I am learning the names of the Austrians:
Gunther, Robert, Irmigarde, Heinz
Hedwig, Siegfried, Albert, Herbert, Gisela
I tumble into bed in a converted barn
Log ceilings and stone walls
Scallop shells and blue tile stars
in the yellow plaster
Lovingly smoothed by hand

April 6 • Day 29
PIEROS TO VEGA DE VALCARCE
15 MILES

Dreaming of Hot Chestnuts

Rain
Mountains
Mist
Fog
Heather
Gorse
Pine
Steep up
Chill
Damp
Austrians
Cheerful
Steep down
Untended groves
Chestnuts scattered on the ground
Remembering my dad
And chestnuts by the fire
Lunch stop
Plates of spaghetti
Wine
Back into rain
Steep up
A Brazilian albergue for the night
Cold inside
We can see our breath
One heater for thirty beds
Huddled in blankets in front of the fire

A stuffed parrot on the wall
mocks the dripping jackets
and gloves hanging to dry
Herbert with the round glasses from Austria
buys me a glass of red wine
I am warm again

Into Galicia

On the 30th day
I walk into Galicia
Last province on the Camino
Land of mountains, rain, Celtic traditions
Home of Santiago de Compostela
It is a day of companionship
Walking up the steep hill
with Armin the Burgmeister
Passing cows with horns, red-breasted birds,
Brook, heather, gorse in the snow
At lunch at the Bar de Mary
I have green tea, and then,
urged by the Austrians,
caña con limón, beer with lemonade
"Good for energy!" they tell me
We hike up to O'Cebreiro, hidden in fog
Visit the old Romanesque church
Then lunch, local Gallego soup
And two glasses of wine
Flying the next three miles to Hospital de la Condesa
and a last supper with the Austrians
Soup, pork chops, dessert
Local cheese with honey
Strong orujo drink
To Albert, one of the older Austrians
who has been so kind to me
I give a chile ristra pin from New Mexico

North Atlantic Ocean

Santiago de Compostela

La Coruña

Arca O Pino

Arzúa

Remonde

Morgade

Gonzar

Samos

Sarria

Triacastela

Hospital de la Condesa

Vega de Valcarce

Molinaseca

Foncebadón

Pieros

Murias de Rechivaldo

Villar de Mazarife

Hospital de Órbigo

León

El Burgo Ranero

Sahagún

Mansilla de las Mulas

Terradillos de los Templarios

Carrión de los Condes

Boadilla del Camino

Castrojeriz

Hornillos del Camino

Burgos

San Juan de Ortega

Tosantos

Santo Domingo de la Calzada

Grañón

Ventosa

Logroño

Torres del Río

Estella

Puente la Reina

Pamplona

Zubiri

Roncesvalles

St Jean Pied de Porte

Bay of Biscay

FRANCE

NAVARRA

LA RIOJA

GALICIA

Lugo

León

Palencia

Burgos

CASTILLA Y LEÓN

SPAIN

PORTUGAL

100 km

0

100 Miles

67

April 8 • Day 31
HOSPITAL DE LA CONDESA TO TRIACASTELA
10 MILES

Easter

It is Easter Sunday
The Austrians walk
reciting a traditional liturgy
The day is cold, the path glorious
Mountains after mountains
their valleys in fog
Walking down the hillside
I delight in green fields below
The sun on my back
Passing stone hedges
Heather
Gorse
Frost, violets
I sing with my friend, Irmi
Spring is arriving.

In a small village
An old woman comes out to greet us
A plate piled high with fresh crepes
sprinkled with powdered sugar
An Easter communion with the pilgrims
My friends depart today
We celebrate our last meal together
with Galician treats: fish croquettes
Apple torte
In the afternoon in Triacastela
in a stone church dedicated to Santiago
we speak our gratitude for this shared Camino time
Irmi gives me a blue ribbon for my pack
And Robert, the band leader, a CD of his band music
My heart is full; I will miss them.

North Atlantic Ocean

Santiago de Compostela

La Coruña

Arca O Pino

Arzúa

Remonde

Morgade

Gonzar

Samos

Sarria

Triacastela

Pieros

Molinaseca

Foncebadón

Murias de Rechivaldo

Hospital de la Condesa

Vega de Valcarce

Hospital de Órbigo

Villar de Mazarife

León

Terradillos de los Templarios

El Burgo Ranero

Sahagún

Mansilla de las Mulas

Carrión de los Condes

Boadilla del Camino

Castrojeriz

Hornillos del Camino

Burgos

San Juan de Ortega

Tosantos

Santo Domingo de la Calzada

Grañón

Ventosa

Logroño

Torres del Río

Estella

Puente la Reina

Pamplona

Zubiri

Roncesvalles

St Jean Pied de Port

Bay of Biscay

GALICIA

Lugo

León

Palencia

Burgos

LA RIOJA

NAVARRA

FRANCE

CASTILLA Y LEÓN

SPAIN

PORTUGAL

100 km

0   100 Miles

TRIACASTELA TO SAMOS
6 MILES

Walking Meditation

A day of walking meditation
I have walked for more than four weeks
I have walked in all weather
alone and with companions
My husband will arrive in two days
for the last week of walking
And I am aware that my pilgrimage will change

I take my time today, walking alone
Savoring the sunshine, the early morning mists
The fruit trees in blossom,
the woods full of bird song
The dappled paths like tunnels
under old chestnuts
The running brooks
Fields of tall green leaves
for the nourishing Galician soup

I find a cracked bird's egg, blue,
Sign of new life
I take a picture to send to my mother
Stop on a bench in the sun for bread and cheese
Tomorrow it will rain
And I want to bask
In each spring and sun-filled moment

After a while
I see below me the monastery of Samos
One of the oldest in the western world
I spend the afternoon next to the río Oribio
Listening to bird song
Watching the crows and a wagtail

Domus Itineris
Pensión Rural
SAMOS (Enfrente Mosteiro S. Xulián)
www.domusitineris.com
Telf.: 982 54 60 88

Reflecting on my journey
Gathering and giving thanks
for all of the blessings of this time
In the evening, I sit at Vespers
surrounded by Benedictine chant
sleep under the sound of ancient bells.

April 10 • Day 33
SAMOS TO SARRIA
8 MILES

Solo

Today is my last day of walking alone
I only have eight miles to walk today
And I linger in these solitary moments
reflecting on a month of pilgrimage.

The rain and wind are steady and cold
In Galicia, land of Celtic influence
Steep rolling hills, green valleys
The track ahead is damp and brown
between banks full of brambles
The trees mossy
dripping with rain
I am chilled
my gloves are wet
my thin blue poncho whips about me,
all noise and little protection from the steady rain,
Yet I do not want to hurry on this last day
Tomorrow my solo pilgrimage will change
to a time of walking with my husband
I look forward to seeing him after five weeks
But I know my walk will be different

In a bar, I am the sole customer
The woman makes me a fresh tortilla patata
The smell of hot oil fills the room
as I warm myself over hot tea.
Later, I climb the stone steps
through the town of Sarria

Finding an albergue with a garden
Next door an Italian restaurant for supper
Sicilians who have immigrated to Spain.
I spend the evening in front of an open fire
Sharing sweet wine and pilgrim stories
with Spaniards José Luis, his son, and four bicyclists
They wish me a Buen Camino
with my husband tomorrow.
Both roads are good.

Together Looking Out

Milagro! In the middle of Galicia, Spain
The bus arrives and my husband alights
He does not speak Spanish
But has found his way here
all the way from Nuevo Mexico
We get the stamp for his passport
the start of his own Camino
He is a pilgrim now, too
We walk in the rain and mist
Catching up after weeks apart
We stop for tea, hot cocoa, and bocadillas
Next to us, a Frenchman who walks 40 kilometers a day
has wine with his lunch
The bar is playing Galician Celtic music
We walk on, companions in the rain
Past mossy stone walls, a new colt
Green fields, rabbits, many birds
We stay the night in Morgade
Have tea in a sitting room
with stone walls and red cushions
and a view over the hills of tomorrow's walk
We sit together looking out.

Morgade
11-4-12

North Atlantic Ocean

Santiago de Compostela

La Coruña

Arca O Pino

Arzúa

Remonde

Morgade

Gonzar

Samos

Sarria

Triacastela

Hospital de la Condesa

Vega de Valcarce

Fonçebadón

Molinaseca

Piéros

Murias de Rechivaldo

Hospital de Órbigo

Villar de Mazarife

León

El Burgo Ranero

Sahagún

Terradillos de los Templarios

Carrión de los Condes

Boadilla del Camino

Castrojeriz

Hornillos del Camino

Burgos

San Juan de Ortega

Tosantos

Santo Domingo de la Calzada

Grañón

Ventosa

Logroño

Torres del Río

Estella

Puente la Reina

Pamplona

Zubiri

Roncesvalles

St Jean Pied de Port

Bay of Biscay

GALICIA

Lugo

León

Mansilla de las Mulas

Palencia

Burgos

CASTILLA Y LEÓN

NAVARRA

LA RIOJA

FRANCE

SPAIN

PORTUGAL

100 km

0   100 Miles

MORGADE TO GONZAR
11 MILES

Two

Alive in the springtime
Up and down hills
A freshly washed sky
with soft white clouds
The path winds through old hamlets
with yellow arrows
on the corners of stone buildings
to mark the way
The day is filled with wildflowers
A cuckoo calls in the wood
At lunch in a restaurant high on a hill
overlooking a valley
Swallows swoop past the windows
The rain pours down outside
As we eat our hot Gallego soup
And fresh greens piled high on the plate
with olives, tuna, tomato, boiled egg
In the afternoon we walk five miles more
Heathered hills, manure-covered fields
remind us we are in rich farm country
We enjoy our dinner of ham and boiled cod
While the women who run the place
Are mesmerized by the soap opera on TV
The shower feels good on my tired body
And two pilgrims fall asleep in a double bed.

Casa García
Gonzar nº 8
Portomarín
K82
Tel.: 982 15 78 42

12. 04. 2012.

North Atlantic Ocean

Santiago de Compostela
La Coruña
Arca O Pino
Arzúa
Remonde
Morgade
Gonzar
Samos
Sarria
Triacastela
Vega de Valcarce
Pieros
Molinaseca
Foncebadón
Murias de Rechivaldo
Hospital de Órbigo
Villar de Mazarife
León
El Burgo Ranero
Sahagún
Hospital de la Condesa
Terradillos de los Templarios
Carrión de los Condes
Boadilla del Camino
Castrojeriz
Hornillos del Camino
Burgos
San Juan de Ortega
Tosantos
Santo Domingo de la Calzada
Grañón
Ventosa
Logroño
Torres del Río
Estella
Puente la Reina
Pamplona
Zubiri
Roncesvalles
St Jean Pied de Port

Bay of Biscay

FRANCE

GALICIA
Lugo
León
Mansilla de las Mulas
Palencia
Burgos
NAVARRA
LA RIOJA

CASTILLA Y LEÓN

S P A I N

100 km
0   100 Miles

PORTUGAL

Rain in Spain

A day in hilly, verdant country
The leaves are budding a soft green
We stop every few hours
for tea, hot chocolate,
Lentil soup for lunch while it rains outside.
It is nice to walk on this cool day
Past farms, on narrow paths between stone walls
Under a huge oak tree
we pause at a worn cross from the 1600s
After fifteen miles we stop
at a rural albergue
with a warm wood fire
A room with heat
and its own shower
I rest, write, the rain pours down
My husband happily makes a foray
to explore a nearby 14th-century castle
The keeper forgets he is there
locks him in at dusk
Bob crawls out a window
His own Camino adventure.

ALBERGUE
A Bolboreta
Vilar de R...monde - PALAS DE REI (Lugo)
13-04-12

North Atlantic Ocean

Santiago de Compostela

La Coruña

Arca O Pino

Arzúa

Remonde

Morgade

Gonzar

Samos

Sarria

Triacastela

GALICIA

Lugo

Vega de Valcarce

Molinaseca

Ponferrada

Foncebadón

Hospital de la Condesa

Murias de Rechivaldo

Hospital de Órbigo

Villar de Mazarife

León

Mansilla de las Mulas

El Burgo Ranero

Sahagún

Terradillos de los Templarios

Carrión de los Condes

Boadilla del Camino

Castrojeriz

Hornillos del Camino

Burgos

San Juan de Ortega

Tosantos

Santo Domingo de la Calzada

Grañón

Ventosa

Logroño

Torres del Río

Estella

Puente la Reina

Pamplona

Zubiri

Roncesvalles

St Jean Pied de Port

Bay of Biscay

FRANCE

NAVARRA

LA RIOJA

Palencia

Burgos

León

CASTILLA Y LEÓN

SPAIN

PORTUGAL

100 km

0   100 Miles

Where We Find Joy

This is Galicia
It is spring; it is green and wet
It rains most of the day
sometimes a downpour
I wear a thin blue poncho
over a rain jacket and rain pants
and waterproof boots
trying to stay dry
A group of teenage pilgrims races past us
They have plastic bags tied around their feet
And jump in all the puddles they can find
Clearly, I have lost the joy in puddle jumping

On this my third-to-last day
I am in no hurry to arrive
I enjoy the songs of blackbirds and robins
The flowering trees
The fields of giant greens
that make Gallego soup
The rain clouds hang over each next rise
Whenever the sunlight breaks through, we stop
Celebrate that it is not raining
Take each other's pictures
with the sun on our faces

North Atlantic Ocean

Santiago de Compostela

La Coruña

Arca O Pino

Arzúa

Remonde

Morgade

Gonzar

Sarria

Samos

Triacastela

Pieros

Vega de Valcarce

Molinaseca

Foncebadón

Murias de Rechivaldo

Hospital de Rechivaldo

Villar de Mazarife

León

El Burgo Ranero

Terradillos de los Templarios

Carrión de los Condes

Sahagún

Boadilla del Camino

Castrojeriz

Hornillos del Camino

Burgos

San Juan de Ortega

Tosantos

Santo Domingo de la Calzada

Grañón

Ventosa

Logroño

Torres del Río

Estella

Puente la Reina

Pamplona

Zubiri

Roncesvalles

St Jean Pied de Port

Bay of Biscay

Hospital de la Condesa

Mansilla de las Mulas

GALICIA

Lugo

León

Palencia

Burgos

NAVARRA

LA RIOJA

CASTILLA Y LEÓN

SPAIN

PORTUGAL

F R A N C E

100 km

0   100 Miles

Living Water

In late afternoon
We stop at a hamlet along the river
We watch a fisherman
And two girls dipping their toes in the water
We could stop here; the albergue
is one of the oldest pilgrim hospitals still standing
We push open the door to the dark, windowless dormitory
It is full of napping pilgrims
and the scent of tired bodies and wet clothes
We decide to walk two more miles.
That evening, a professor from a local university
goes out of her way
to lead us to a family restaurant
We eat our fill of salad,
Rice, fried eggs, stewed beef, boiled potatoes
And mushroom omelette
Fall into bed, sleep.

North Atlantic Ocean

Santiago de Compostela
La Coruña
Arca O Pino
Arzúa
Remonde
Morgade
Gonzar
Sarria
Samos
Triacastela
Hospital de la Condesa
Vega de Valcarce
Murias de Rechivaldo
Pieros
Molinaseca
Foncebadón
Hospital de Órbigo
Villar de Mazarife
León
El Burgo Ranero
Sahagún
Mansilla de las Mulas
Terradillos de los Templarios
Carrión de los Condes
Boadilla del Camino
Castrojeriz
Hornillos del Camino
Burgos
San Juan de Ortega
Tosantos
Santo Domingo de la Calzada
Grañón
Ventosa
Logroño
Torres del Río
Estella
Puente la Reina
Pamplona
Zubiri
Roncesvalles
St Jean Pied de Port

Bay of Biscay

GALICIA
Lugo
León
Palencia
Burgos
LA RIOJA
NAVARRA
FRANCE

CASTILLA Y LEÓN

SPAIN

PORTUGAL

100 km
0
100 Miles

Arrival

Our last day dawns sunny with fog
The ivy-covered old growth trees
hold their branches over us
An archway for us to walk through
as the narrow lanes carry us to Santiago.
At the overlook to the city
the pilgrim statue is under repair
covered in scaffolding. I look down
at the towers of the cathedral in the distance
It does not seem real
that my feet have actually carried me
all this way, five hundred miles.

Almost reluctant, I walk down the steps
into the city that has welcomed pilgrims
for a millennium
We stop in a bar
to eat the famous octopus at a long wooden table
Pour red wine from a pitcher
Then walk through the old city center
to the cathedral
its steps and columns worn
by pilgrims' grateful feet and hands
Such outpourings of prayers
are held by these stones
I am sad, glad, full, empty
Finished, and beginning
Trying to hold it all

RESTAURANTE

Tangueiro

P U L P E R I A

1 6 ABR. 2012

North Atlantic Ocean

Santiago de Compostela
La Coruña
Arca O Pino
Arzúa
Remonde
Morgade
Gonzar
Samos
Sarria
Triacastela
GALICIA
Lugo
Hospital de la Condesa
Molinaseca
Foncebadón
Ponferrada
Vega de Valcarce
Murias de Rechivaldo
Hospital de Órbigo
Villar de Mazarife
León
León
El Burgo Ranero
Sahagún
Terradillos de los Templarios
Mansilla de las Mulas
Carrión de los Condes
Boadilla del Camino
Palencia
Castrojeriz
Hornillos del Camino
Burgos
San Juan de Ortega
Tosantos
Santo Domingo de la Calzada
Grañón
Ventosa
Logroño
Torres del Río
LA RIOJA
Estella
Puente la Reina
Pamplona
NAVARRA
Zubiri
Roncesvalles
St Jean Pied de Port
Bay of Biscay
FRANCE

100 km
0   100 Miles

CASTILLA Y LEÓN

SPAIN

PORTUGAL

85

Benediction

We are blessed again;
Today they will swing the botafumeiro
It was once used at each pilgrim mass
but now there is a charge
We learn that a group from another country
has paid the fee

Waiting, we sit in silence in the wooden pew
A choir sings
We watch as the men in maroon robes
Unleash the heavy braided ropes
Lower the large silver botafumeiro
to the place near the altar
Where the priest loads the coals and the incense,
sets it swinging
The men pull the ropes to raise it high
give it momentum
As the powerful organ plays
the heavy silver urn flies high above us
Up toward the arched stone
through shafts of filtered sunlight
The sweet smoke of incense
drifting down,
Balm and benediction

North Atlantic Ocean

Santiago de Compostela
La Coruña
Arca O Pino
Arzúa
Remonde
Morgade
Gonzar
Samos
Sarria
Triacastela
Pieros
Vega de Valcarce
Molinaseca
Foncebadón
Hospital de la Condesa
Murias de Rechivaldo
Villar de Mazarife
Hospital de Órbigo
León
El Burgo Ranero
Sahagún
Mansilla de las Mulas
Terradillos de los Templarios
Carrión de los Condes
Boadilla del Camino
Castrojeriz
Hornillos del Camino
Burgos
San Juan de Ortega
Tosantos
Santo Domingo de la Calzada
Grañón
Ventosa
Logroño
Torres del Río
Estella
Puente la Reina
Pamplona
Zubiri
Roncesvalles
St. Jean Pied de Port

Bay of Biscay

FRANCE

GALICIA
Lugo
León
Palencia
Burgos
NAVARRA
LA RIOJA

CASTILLA Y LEÓN

SPAIN

PORTUGAL

100 km
0   100 Miles

SETTING OUT FROM SANTIAGO DE COMPOSTELA

The Path Home

Rustic grilled bread
Drizzled with olive oil
Piled with crushed tomatoes
And fresh cheese
Café con leche.
I savor, linger
It is the last breakfast in Spain
Preparation for the day's journey
This time by taxi and plane

Ah, how I will miss these tastes
The bread freshly sliced
The espresso just drawn.
My feet already miss being on the dirt road
But the next journey calls
I give thanks for the way
For God, for all of the human mercies
That have brought me to this path.

Flying to Madrid
We cross over the Camino
where pilgrims walk below
hidden by the clouds
All travelers disappear into spirit
in the mists of time
and other pilgrims follow
We are all walking toward God.

Spirit of the Camino

SHARE WHAT YOU HAVE WITH OTHER PILGRIMS.

LIVE IN THE MOMENT.

WATCH FOR THE SIGNS THAT YOU ARE ON THE PATH.
WELCOME ALL THAT COMES TO YOU.

SENSE THE PRAYERS OF THOSE WHO HAVE GONE
BEFORE YOU, LEAVE GOOD WILL BEHIND FOR THOSE
WHO WILL COME AFTER YOU, APPRECIATE YOUR
COMPANIONS WHO WALK WITH YOU.

CARE FOR THE ALBERGUE AS IF IT WERE YOUR
OWN HOME.

GIVE THANKS AT THE END OF EACH DAY.

WHEN YOU ARRIVE IN SANTIAGO, EMBRACE
THE SAINT ON BEHALF OF THOSE UNABLE TO
MAKE THE PILGRIMAGE.

NOTE: TO OBTAIN THE COMPOSTELA IN SANTIAGO, PILGRIMS
MUST COMPLETE THE FINAL 100 KILOMETERS IF ON FOOT,
OR THE FINAL 200 KILOMETERS IF ON BICYCLE

Credencial del Peregrino

16 ABR. 2012

About the Author

Sarah Kotchian, EdM, MPH, PhD, is a writer, artist, mother of two grown children, and retired public health administrator. Trained in spiritual direction at the Hesychia School of Spiritual Direction and a candidate for lay minister in the Presbyterian church, she facilitates workshops and contemplative retreats using creative writing and art. She completed a 500-mile solo pilgrimage on the Camino de Santiago in Spain in 2012. She and her husband live in New Mexico. She may be contacted at skotchian@comcast.net.

CPSIA information can be obtained
at www.ICGtesting.com
Printed in the USA
LVIC06n0824061214
417472LV00003B/3

* 9 7 8 0 6 9 2 3 3 6 3 2 8 *